Traveling Solo?

75 Winning Tips for Solo Travelers

Claudia Kielich

Contents

Also by Claudia Kielich   v
Epigraph   ix
Introduction   xi

Part One
TRAVELING SOLO

1. GIRL SCOUTS - BE PREPARED   3
2. PLANNING   5
3. PACKING   7
4. PREPARATION   11
5. TRANSPORTATION   13
6. HOTEL   17
7. DINING   19
8. MONEY   21
9. SHOPPING   23
10. LOST   25
11. SAFETY   27
12. PANIC ATTACK   29
13. TIPPING   31
14. MOST IMPORTANT TIP   33

Part Two
SENIOR TIPS

15. TAXI, UBER, LYFT   37
16. AVOID THE AVOIDABLE   39
17. KNOW YOUR NEIGHBORHOOD   41
18. PHYSICAL PREPARATION   43
19. ADHERE TO LOCAL REGULATIONS   45
20. RESPECT THE LOCAL ENVIRONMENT   47
21. ACT YOUR AGE   49
22. STAY IN RHYTHM   51
23. GIVE YOURSELF A BREAK   53

24. BE FLEXIBLE	55
25. CAUTION - AIRPORTS	57

Part Three
BONUS TRAVEL TIPS

26. ITINERARIES	61
27. SURVIVAL PHRASES	63
28. FLIGHTS, FERRIES AND TRAINS	65
29. HOTELS	67
30. LOCAL CONTACTS, ADDRESSES AND PHONE NUMBERS	69
31. RESTAURANT AND FOOD RECOMMENDATIONS	71
32. PLACES OF INTEREST	73
33. DAILY EXPENSES	75
34. NEW FRIENDS	77
35. GIFTS AND SOUVENIRS	79
36. TRIP MEMORIES	81
37. DAILY THOUGHTS	83
About the Author	85

Also by Claudia Kielich

GREEK ISLAND ADVENTURES Escapades for the Sophisticated Traveler

Dedicated to all of you Adventure Seekers.

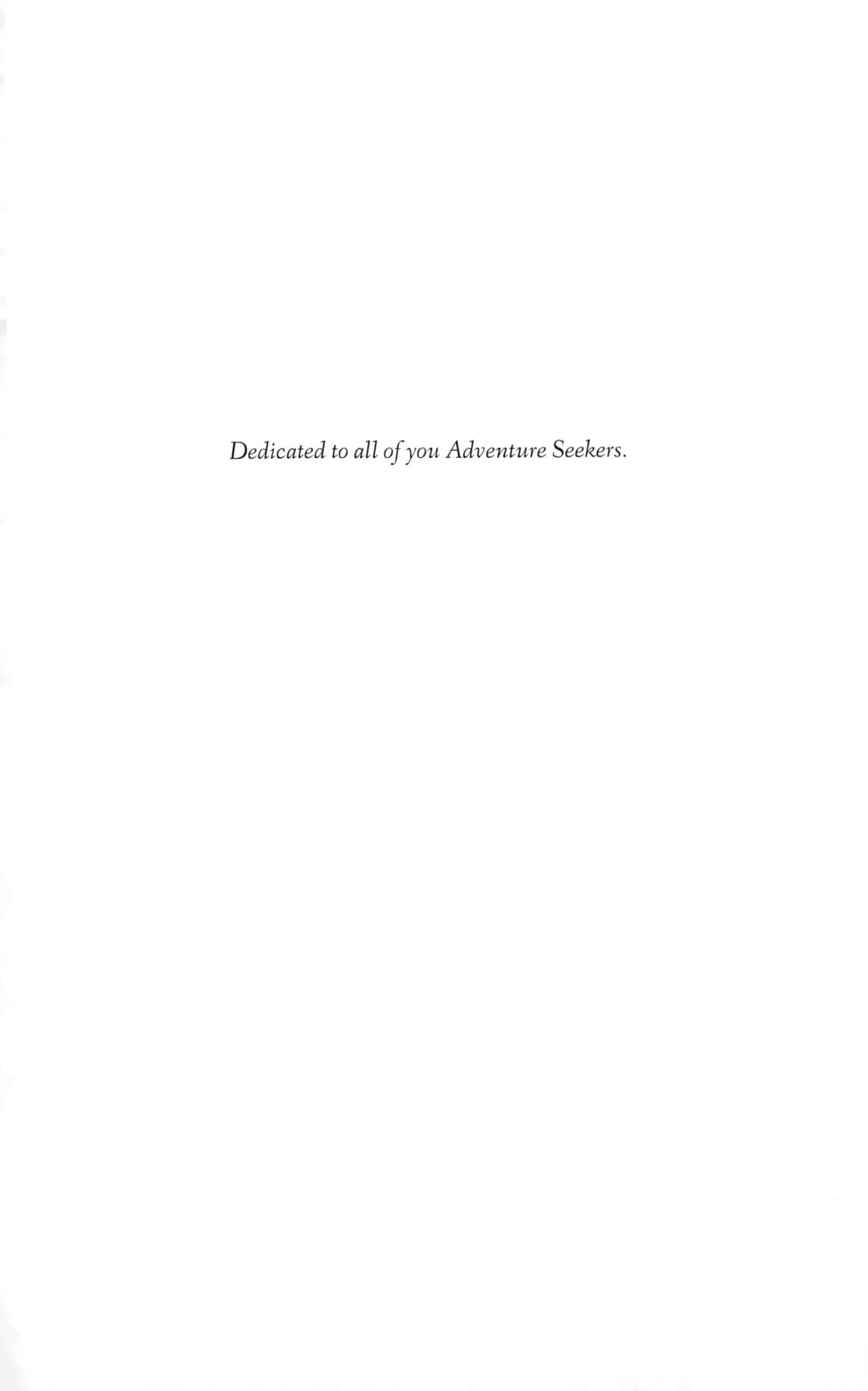

"Nothing must be postponed. Take time by the forelock. Now or never! You must live in the present, launch yourself on every wave, find your eternity in each moment."

Henry David Thoreau - American Renaissance Thinker

Introduction

Be true to yourself. Choose your destination wisely and find what is a good fit for you. That thoughtful decision is half of feeling self-confident and safe on any trip. Go for a few days or a week, no more. Treat yourself. Don't be cheap. Check out your budget and what wonderful options there are out there just for you.

Be cautious of naysayers. Cover your ears. Everyone will be a bit jealous of your zeal and independence. Go for it. The best part of traveling solo is you begin to recognize your own best friend, yourself.

The journey will take many different forks in the road. That's what makes solo travel exciting and magical.

People are always open to one individual. When there are two people, they seem to ignore you since you are already fine. The person who stands out traveling solo emanates curiosity, adventure and self-confidence. Fellow travelers want to know you and service people want to protect you. It's just human nature.

I found, in my solo travel of over 20 years in business and for pleasure, my most special moments were when I trusted myself and my environment. Travel with joy and grace and you will attract protection and love wherever your travels take you.

Carpe Diem - Seize the Day!

Part One

TRAVELING SOLO

Chapter 1

GIRL SCOUTS - BE PREPARED

Having been an executive for the National Organization of Girl Scouts in New York City, I've traveled solo using some of my tips from my Girl Scout days. Seriously, when lost in New Mexico, in the Los Alamos State Park, I was able to retrace our movements because I set up a rock path on our way into the forest. Two bikers discovered us as the sun was setting and went for help.

In Denver, when visiting my sister, with a Girl Scout colleague, we were stuck on a cliff in an ice storm and couldn't get traction under our tires. I remembered when we were Brownies, we made a weaved mat called a sit-upon out of newspapers that would keep us dry when sitting on the ground. Luckily, we found a cardboard box in the trunk and made a sit-upon. Sure enough, it had enough traction to get our car out of that ditch.

Don't forget your past skills you acquired throughout your childhood. They are basic and come in handy.

. . .

All of us have memories that kick in when we have a gut feeling that arises when we are faced with an emergency. Nothing is ever wasted in life experiences.

Chapter 2
PLANNING

Research your own comfort zone for example, mega hotels, resorts, ranches, or smaller hotels and charming neighborhoods. For instance, I am completely overwhelmed by Las Vegas, but comfortable walking in a Temple in Greece.

Only plan a weekend or week trip for your first solo trip. A place that you never have been but close enough to get home if you change your mind mid-trip.

Cover your ears when you share with friends and family you are planning to travel solo or you will never do it.

Check your budget and never pay more than you can afford. The guilt will eventually set in either on the trip or upon arrival of the credit card statement.

. . .

Take a CPR Course at a local Firehouse. Learn the Heimlich Maneuver on yourself.

Go to your local library or google the language of the country you are visiting. Make a Survival Phrases list that includes bathroom, how much, and police.

Always buy travel insurance.

Chapter 3
PACKING

Don't take anything you really care about.

Don't take jewelry. Buy costume jewelry in souvenir stores and have fun.

Squish your clothes in plastic baggies and you'll have more space.

Take a cheap computer or use a hotel computer. Pack an old-fashioned bandana. You'd be surprised how handy it is if you get overheated and need to cool down with water on your head or neck, for surprise spills, and also cleaning an accidental wound.

Make a generic list of your medicines so the pharmacy in the country you are visiting will be able to look them up. If you require medical or dental services, you will be asked for a list of your current meds. Have it handy.

Be prepared to throw stuff out.

I actually did this. The airline I was flying to Greece allowed 35 pounds in a carry-on.

    Upon checking in at the ticketing desk, I was told that my carry-on was 37 pounds and only 35 pounds were allowed, so I needed to pay $80 for the extra weight. I didn't blink an eye and asked where the closest garbage can was. Before the agent could answer, I noticed one nearby and began walking toward it. The agent stepped onto the suitcase scale and ran up to me with a ticket and told me to go to the gate.

Don't waste your money on unimportant things that you packed.

Something similar happened to me in a prior communist country. Upon leaving the country, my hosts told me at the airport that once I walked through the glass doors without them, I was no longer protected. The agents went through my belongings and asked for what was equivalent to $300 in rubles to let me take my possessions including souvenirs. I told them I seriously did not have the rubles since I spent all of my money on my last day prior to leaving for the airport. I said they could keep my luggage and began walking toward the gate. They knew there were cameras everywhere and they were extorting me, so they quickly packed everything up and off I went with my friends cheering me on through the glass doors.

. . .

Don't argue with authorities.

Chapter 4

PREPARATION

Make a copy of credit cards, passport, license, any important info and give to a friend or family member. You can always contact them if you need to cancel credit cards.

Safety begins with peace of mind. Tie a ribbon or belt on your suitcase so you can identify it throughout your travels. I use a red braided dog collar which clamps onto other things, like a computer bag or backpack, when in the airport. This prevents your suitcase from being picked up by mistake and it's also easy to identify if it floats in the overhead bin or is packed together with other bags on the turnstile.

When departing the house, count the items you will be carrying on your trip. Purse, computer case, backpack, carry-on suitcase, and checked baggage are the most likely.

. . .

Arriving at the airport, count again when you get out of the car or taxi, count again at check-in, count again after going through TSA, and count again when you arrive at your seat on the plane.

Do not put your computer in the overhead bin. Put it on your lap or between your legs under your seat.

Make sure you are wearing a money belt under your clothes for large amounts of money, credit cards (don't take more than two), and driver's license.

Make sure your passport, small amount of cash, phone, and reading glasses are readily available in a fanny pack on your waist or a purse with a strap you can anchor with your ankle when you fall asleep.

Chapter 5

TRANSPORTATION

Air

After you check in at the airport, go directly to the TSA and then directly to your gate. Gates change and the last thing you want is to be searching for it at the last minute. It may be a long walk and may not be up yet, but get there no matter what. Once you find it, you can go to the restroom, cafe or store that is nearby that gate, knowing how much time you have to return.

When flying on a small charter, know your destination, know how many stops the plane is making and get off at the appropriate one. In Seville, Spain, working on the World's Fair Opening Ceremonies, I was on my way to the Royal Andalusian Horse Academy on a short flight. I was so excited, I got off the plane on the first stop and didn't realize I was in the wrong city until the taxi driver told me we should return to the airport and try to catch the plane I just left.

Taxi

When entering a taxi, after giving a destination, ask for an approximate cost: $3.00, $30.00 or $300? You'd be surprised how much is lost in translation.

Don't pay until you are out of the taxi and on the street with your luggage and in front of your destination.

Too many people are stranded in unfamiliar neighborhoods because they gave the driver improper directions. For example, every neighborhood has a Main St. If need be, get back into the taxi and regroup.

Do not hail a cab. Always go to a hotel or restaurant and ask for a taxi. The drivers are responsible to that establishment and are vetted. They also are more willing to take you anywhere since they return to that establishment for another fare vs. trolling a neighborhood for a customer.

When leaving a taxi, always look behind you. In London, I left my expensive Yashica camera and because of the "being stupid fee" paid to drivers, almost all lost is found back at the official headquarters.

In Rome, I left my briefcase which included all my travel expenses from a business trip to Japan and Australia. The driver returned it to the hotel to collect the handsome ransom the hotel charges the forgetful guest on their behalf for the return.

Metro

Purchase your tickets at a machine, a kiosk, or from a teller and do not get on a metro without one. I did. In Lyon (France) and Prague (Czech Republic), there are young undercover detectives who watch you and watch your habit of getting on and off when you please. It's difficult to find out where to buy the tickets in some places; however, the humiliation is worth giving it a second thought The young men usually require you to pay up on the spot, depending on how many days and nights you have been hopping on and off or they ask you to leave the metro with them and go to the station.

Stand near the door so you don't miss your stop. Usually, the area maps are above the door and if you concentrate enough, you will be able to figure out your stop or ask a fellow passenger. I find that young people, families with kids, and tourists are near the doors.

Bus

Buy tickets in advance. Ask your hotel or local kiosk or cafe.

When boarding a city or tour bus, sit up front. People on the bus are observing you and will let you know if you've left or dropped anything.

Do not take a city bus if you are not prepared to jump off and on quickly. In Indonesia the buses leave the doors open and merely slow down for exiting and entering, never really stopping.

On a tour bus, sit next to someone and not alone. This way you have someone to watch your things if need be. Make a friend. Bring them a coffee or bottle of water for watching your things.

Ferry

Use local Travel Agencies for your ferry tickets. This way, you won't have to stand in lines at the Port. You will have a ticket going to the correct destination and on it will be the dock you will depart from. You will have something from a legitimate agency to show the officials when you are confused or challenged.

Do not let anyone carry your bags for you.

Don't pack anything you really care about. Ferries bundle all the luggage together in a storage location near the automobiles and trucks. When departing the ferry, there is a flurry of activity and it may be picked up by mistake, usually by another tourist.

Sit next to non-smokers, families and most of all, silver haired older ladies. They will watch your things for you. They will even watch out for you without you even asking. It's even better when you find two or more silver haired older ladies.

On a ferry, keep checking the schedule for your stop. The stops are fast and once you are off you can't get back on. Once on land, make sure you check the ferry schedule for the return ferry so you don't miss it. Sometimes your ferry may return to a different dock, which can be confusing.

In St. Petersburg, Russia, when choosing a ferry that passed all the old palaces along the river, I got on one going up river, not down. Since I took this ferry the day before I did not recognize landmarks I had made for myself. I immediately listened carefully for anyone who spoke English and when I found a gentleman who did, he notified the captain for me. They arranged to drop me off at the next port and have a taxi waiting for me to take me back to my hotel.

Chapter 6

HOTEL

Upon arrival, count your items. Be sure your passport is returned to you at the front desk with your key.

When getting on an elevator and you feel uncomfortable because it's late and you're alone, get off and ask the front desk to have a bellman escort you to your room.

Check your floor when you get on the elevator for ease and comfort walking to and from your room. Are you walking around a corner? How many other rooms are on the floor? Check for signs for easy exit or ice machine, fire extinguisher, or maids closet.

When entering your room, turn the lights off. Turn the video camera on your phone on and do a sweep of the room or rooms, looking for a red laser light. This will pick up any hidden camera.

. . .

When putting your items in the room safe, put one of your shoes in with your items. This will help you remember to retrieve your items since you will need your shoe.

Immediately take a brisk walk through your neighborhood (daytime only) and look for landmarks like a restaurant awning, dry cleaners, antique shop, cafe, something unusual, not a common fruit or vegetable stand. When visiting larger international cities neighborhoods tend to look alike.

Carry the card of the hotel with you at all times. There is usually a phone number and a map on the back if you get turned around.

When staying at a rural, small, or island hotel with limited security, line up a glass, soda bottle, beer bottle or wine bottle in front of the door before going to bed. If someone mistakenly tries to enter, the noise will scare them away. That's a tip from my Dad, when we would visit motels on vacation as kids. He did it with Coke bottles. We laughed, but it worked when some young fellow I met at the pool earlier wanted my phone number.

Chapter 7
DINING

When dining alone, ask for a table for two. There are no tables for one and you will not stick out like a sore thumb. Other diners will not notice you are dining alone. Once two menus are placed on the table, take a look and when the waiter returns say that you will go ahead with your meal even though your guest has not arrived.

Don't order a lot of food. Start small. Many cultures have one dish for 2-4 people and more than once the waiter is too busy to mention this. You can always order more if you are still hungry.

When asked, always tell people, such as a waiter, sales clerk, other tourists, taxi drivers and hotel employees that you are in town visiting a friend or family member. Make it up if you have to, since it always makes for easy conversation and the fact that you are traveling solo never comes up in conversations with strangers.

Check out a local taverna, cafe, bar or restaurant and frequent it regularly. You will get to know the staff and see others who are regulars. It's a good feeling to have a go-to hangout and people you can check in with.

Never order or accept an unfamiliar cocktail. You may suffer from a reaction to it.

I was sick for two days in Costa Rica after having a pretty green drink that I thought was a margarita. It was a local drink that was mixed with unknown ingredients.

On the overnight train from Odessa to Yalta, Ukraine, I was invited to participate in a social event enjoying the Russian tradition of drinking a Bloody Mary. First, in a tall glass, a lemon is squeezed in the bottom, then tomato juice is added and a knife is inserted into the mixture with vodka pouring down the knife, which goes straight to the bottom of the drink. Again, sick for two days.

While dining in local street markets or stopping for a beverage at a kiosk, do not drink from cups or open containers of anything. Always order a bottle of water, soda or beer, open it yourself or watch it being opened and drink it with a straw. I actually carry two metal travel straws.

When ordering bottled water, make sure the bottle is brought to the table and opened in front of you. Listen for the snap of the cap to guarantee it was not refilled with tap water.

Chapter 8
MONEY

When making a purchase or engaged in any money transaction, don't talk too much about other things and concentrate on what you are doing. Mistakes are made when there are too many distractions.

Always keep a $100 bill folded neatly in a gum wrapper in case you lose your wallet or purse. Put it in the rim of your hat, your shoe or somewhere else that you won't think about it too much.

Ask for the price in advance of a purchase and write it down if need be. I spent $300 at a hairdresser's shop in Rome instead of $30, all because I kept saying si, si, si to whatever they were upselling.

How not to go over budget. Keep in mind the price you are paying for something, especially impulsive buys, and double it in your head. My brother-in-law, Spiros, taught me this bit of wisdom and saved me a boatload of money. The final number usually brings you back to reality.

Always have enough money for a taxi and one night in a nice hotel to leave an uncomfortable situation. You will calm down and be able to call family and friends.

Chapter 9
SHOPPING

Always ask how much an item is. If it's on sale, ask what the reduced price is. Ask for the price to be translated in dollars if you still don't understand.

When in Japan, I needed a new makeup brush and visited a nice department store. I purchased the brush with Japanese currency and later found out it was $180.

When in Paris at the Georges V Hotel, a martini at the time cost $10.00 and the nuts that accompanied the drink were $19.

When in a crowded souvenir store filled with youngsters off buses, go to the front of the line and ask if you can pay first. Usually, you don't have to get in line and are purchasing more expensive items.

Chapter 10

LOST

Don't roam. Walk with intent even when window shopping.

If you find yourself in a city, town or village where the language barrier is too extreme, and you are feeling alone, go to a local kiosk, hotel, souvenir or grocery store and buy postcards of all the sites you would like to visit. Go to a local hotel and ask for a taxi. Give the postcards to the driver and ask him to spend the day with you. I did this in Budapest, Hungary, years ago and it was not only cost effective but I had my own private driver.

Have a backup plan when Plan A and Plan B fall apart. Plan C will be just as enjoyable. I do this for every outing every day.

If someone asks you for your hotel name, give them the most expensive hotel in the city. You can always go there and get a taxi to your own hotel. This keeps strangers from prying. Don't overshare information.

When there are no hotels in the neighborhood, knock on the door of an office or home and ask the person who answers to call you a taxi. Do not enter the home even if asked. Stay outside.

Chapter 11

SAFETY

Wear a whistle as part of your jewelry. Everyone responds to a whistle.

Always look behind you when leaving a bus, hotel, taxi, cafe or theater. You would be surprised how many times you leave something of value.

When you have a gut feeling you are being followed in an international airport, go to the Airline First Class lounge you are traveling on. I was in Turkey and had quite a long layover when I noticed the same man near me wherever I sat. I went into the First Class lounge and told the receptionist I did not have a First Class ticket but felt I was being followed. She immediately reached into a drawer and pulled out a $50 voucher for a restaurant and told me to stay there until my gate was called and not leave the airport for any reason.

. . .

Never leave your tour group to roam on your own. I was in Panama on an official government tour. While finishing lunch I stepped outside alone for a breath of fresh air. A man on a bus was watching me and got off the bus to approach me. I went straight into a nearby beauty salon and the man got back on the same bus.

Don't push unknown buttons in your hotel room. I was taking a bubble bath in the Shangri La Hotel in Bangkok, Thailand, and pushed a button on the wall next to the tub. In came three men in white tuxedos wearing pink turbans, with shampoo, champagne and fresh warm towels.

Chapter 12

PANIC ATTACK

If you find yourself in a city, town or village and feel lost and alone, don't panic. Go into a local hotel and ask what bus tours are going to where you are staying. You will immediately calm down and feel a sense of security when you meet friendly tourists on the bus.

Churches everywhere are open all day and into the evening except the United States.

Pop into one, light a candle and say a prayer.

When you are scattered and can't think straight, head for the sea, or any body of water nearby. Water calms us. Walk near the water or in the water. Pick up some rocks and hold them in your hands and put them in your pockets. You'd be amazed how this really works!

Chapter 13
TIPPING

Tip, Tip, Tip. I cannot stress enough how important this is. Tip everyone you are expected to tip. The tour guide, the tour bus driver, the interpreter, the waiter, the waitress, the maitre d' who gives you the table with a view, the reception desk clerk or concierge who helped you daily and most of all, the doorman of your hotel if there is one.

The more generous you are on a trip translates to the generosity that comes back to you in so many wonderful ways that you never expected. It makes for a joyful journey.

Chapter 14
MOST IMPORTANT TIP

Give yourself Grace! Give yourself some compassion. Win over self-criticism when you go to sleep every night of your trip.

When you wake up say aloud "today is the happiest day of my life" and it will be.

Part Two
SENIOR TIPS

Chapter 15

TAXI, UBER, LYFT

In any country you find yourself in, when ordering a taxi, uber or lyft on an app on your phone, keep it open when entering the vehicle. Show the driver you will be tracking the vehicle to the desired destinations. I have had the experience in Spain of the driver asking me questions on the route I had chosen and if I wanted to deviate, and of course I didn't know. I just showed the driver the original request on my app. If possible, it's always a good idea to have the person you just left track you on their phone as a backup. If traveling by taxi, always ask the driver to turn on the meter and ask the approximate cost of the trip. If you are aware of the price and it's out of the range ask the driver to stop and get out.

Chapter 16

AVOID THE AVOIDABLE

Never accept rides from strangers or new found friends. My pal Jill just finished a horseback ride on vacation in Italy when she was too cheap to take a taxi back to her hotel. She asked the stable mucker for a ride home and did not realize he had been drinking. After a car crash she ended up in the hospital and then discharged to her hotel. The hotel asked her to leave, since her reservation was for a short period of time, and new guests were arriving. She found this unacceptable and blamed everyone but herself. Tip - Avoid predictable accidents.

Chapter 17
KNOW YOUR NEIGHBORHOOD

Google Map your hotel or airbnb prior to booking, look for hills, local grocery stores and most of all how far it is from taxis and public transportation. You would be surprised how many countries have hills right in the middle of an urban area and you won't be able to walk up your street in your chosen neighborhood.

Chapter 18

PHYSICAL PREPARATION

Prepare yourself physically. Too many Seniors are now taking hiking adventures as their preferred vacation. Make sure you do the same challenging exercise in your neighborhood at home prior to your vacation. On a trip to New Zealand, I was on the famous hiking tour, the Routeburn Walk through the New Zealand Alps. A hiking guide accompanied 2 people at a time and told us the men were never prepared for this walk. The men had to be helicoptered out on a regular basis. Why? Women usually plan the vacation and also prepare themselves physically and mentally for the hike. At the last minute the men usually agree to go along or all along thought they were fit enough for the hike. Make sure you do a dress rehearsal in your hometown. It's a good idea to check in with your doctor prior to departure.

Chapter 19

ADHERE TO LOCAL REGULATIONS

Don't pick anything up for a souvenir. I was in Costa Rica and I consider myself an environmentalist. Our driver stopped at a beach sanctuary for turtles and I thoughtlessly picked up 2 rocks and put them in the back of the jeep. When the driver saw what I did he told me to wrap them up and be prepared to be arrested if I really wanted them. Lesson well learned.

Chapter 20

RESPECT THE LOCAL ENVIRONMENT

Pay attention to the rules of the sun. In Greece, many senior hikers go missing every year while on holiday. They do not take water and they think the sun is similar to their hometown. The result is disaster. My own experience has served me well in keeping by the sun rules of every country I visit. While on holiday in Greece, I chose to stay at a beach restaurant after my Greek pals went home for naps. I swam and then sat under a sheer beach umbrella and needless to say ended up with heatstroke. Never again. I pay attention to what the locals do.

Chapter 21
ACT YOUR AGE

Avoid tours for the young, not the young at heart. While on holiday in Costa Rica with my partner at the time we chose jungle zip lining, where you fly from tree to tree on a zip line. However, the only problem was that my partner, who happened to look exactly like Stephen Segal in size and weight, ended up only half way making it. I zipped right across and he didn't. He stopped in the middle to the shock of the men in charge. I feel they didn't think through the size and weight of an American who had a career in construction. After much panic and discussion, he was given giant leather gloves to protect his hands and asked to pull himself along the line to safety.

Chapter 22
STAY IN RHYTHM

Go to bed early and wake up late. Don't try to be someone you aren't. Keep your schedule that you have at home and relish in the fact you don't have to prove anything to anybody. Nothing really great happens late at night unless you are under 40! Keep yourself healthy and happy. Wake up late and have a good meal. This sets your pace for the day and you will not regret it.

Chapter 23

GIVE YOURSELF A BREAK

Save your energy. Always sit down. Look for walls, benches, cafes, and stairs to sit. I find you are able to regroup and rest. This is a perfect way to get to know the culture. What people are wearing, what they are saying, how many babies go by in strollers, how many old people still have a quick gate and how many tourists are enjoying themselves. It's a joy to rest and not rush.

Chapter 24

BE FLEXIBLE

Have a flexible itinerary. I learned this from my sister who lives in Athens. When I visit, she always has 3 choices every morning. This way if A doesn't work because it may be a holiday, the museum may be closed or it's too hot to go to the city center, we move to plan B and enjoy an afternoon visiting air conditioned churches or enjoying a long lunch at the beach. Plan C is always a good nap!

Chapter 25
CAUTION - AIRPORTS

Do NOT ask strangers to watch your belongings at the airport gate. Always take items with you no matter how many you have. Bathrooms all over the world in airports now are large enough to accommodate you and your carry on.

Part Three
BONUS TRAVEL TIPS

Chapter 26

ITINERARIES

Organize your itineraries in such a way that you can reflect on your trip easily and with enthusiasm. Nothing is ever wasted when traveling and to be conscious of this makes your trip more memorable.

> "There is a kind of magicness about going far away and then coming back all changed." - Kate Douglas Wiggin

Chapter 27

SURVIVAL PHRASES

It's always appreciated by the people of the host countries that you have put in some effort on their behalf to honor them with a few phrases in their own language. This tip goes far in being accepted on so many levels.

> "To speak a language is to take on a world, a culture." - Frantz Fanon

Chapter 28
FLIGHTS, FERRIES AND TRAINS

This is the fun tip. Almost all transportation stresses us out. Plan in advance every move you make and turn it into a challenge. Always keep your transportation schedules in a separate file and check it regularly prior to the trip and on it. Remember the only thing we can really count on in life is change.

My mantra is "this is easy and fun and I will do this with joy!"

"Nothing develops intelligence like travel." - Emile Zola

Chapter 29

HOTELS

Hotels offer us an adventure unto itself. The check in, the room, the restaurants, the bar, the pool, the staff, the spa. I can go on and on. The most important thing is to take full advantage of your hotel from the complimentary breakfast to the cocktail before dinner. Believe it or not, the hotel wants your business and is delighted to make you happy.

> "The Grand Budapest Hotel is not really my thing but I kind of loved it." - Quentin Tarantino

Chapter 30

LOCAL CONTACTS, ADDRESSES AND PHONE NUMBERS

You would be surprised how fast you are making new contacts, from your seat mates on the plane to fellow ferry passengers. Keep a record of these folks because you can always contact them while traveling and make plans to meet up on the trip.

> I met a lot of people in Europe. I even encountered myself." - James Bald

Chapter 31

RESTAURANT AND FOOD RECOMMENDATIONS

Who doesn't love food? Write down where and what you are experiencing in your culinary world. It makes for wonderful conversation throughout your trip and lovely photos on your instagram.

"One's destination is never a place, but a new way of seeing things." - Henry Miller

Chapter 32
PLACES OF INTEREST

Always go out of your way to find a new and interesting tour. Something out of your comfort zone. You will make new friends and feel accomplished.

"My favorite thing is to go where I've never been." - Diane Arbus

Chapter 33
DAILY EXPENSES

It's wise to jot down your daily spending on food, wine and friends. Gifts, souvenirs and admission tickets all add up. For a lengthy vacation don't spend all your money too soon.

Investment in travel is an investment in yourself." - Matthew Karsten

Chapter 34
NEW FRIENDS

Create a database of photos and information of new friends so you can send them photos later and keep in touch. Travel friends are for life and usually invite you to their home in their country if you're lucky.

> "My heart is warm with friends I make, And better friends I'll not be knowing; Yet there isn't a train I wouldn't take No matter where it's going." - Edna St. Vincent Millay

Chapter 35

GIFTS AND SOUVENIRS

Always travel light. I buy a six pack of coasters and give one each to my friends for their water or coffee next to their computer. Not only is this economical but useful. Remember who doesn't love a refrigerator magnet or a wine cork.

Limit your souvenirs to keychains, cheap jewelry or tokens like shot glasses.

"Travel is the only thing you buy that makes you richer." - Anonymous

Chapter 36

TRIP MEMORIES

Keep track of your outstanding moments. The food, the people, the color of the sky and the unexpected gems of each day.

"It is not the destination where you end up but the mishaps and memories you create along the way." - Penelope Riley

Chapter 37

DAILY THOUGHTS

I can't stress this enough. It's important to jot down our feelings, our changes, our new point of view and our love for the experience of the day. I always find a constant state of gratitude brings protection and a sense of wonder for what's next.

> "I love the feeling of being anonymous in a city I've never been before." - Bill Bryson

About the Author

Claudia Kielich is a longtime resident of Venice Beach, California with an executive background in the entertainment and travel industries.

Throughout Claudia's career in international business development for Radio City Music Hall and Universal Studios, she traveled the world producing creative, innovative live entertainment events.

After years of business and pleasure trips, she created her own unique tips to maximize the joys of traveling solo. And she generously shares her own travel experience in her magical best-selling book "GREEK ISLAND ADVENTURES Escapades for the Sophisticated Traveler".

Copyright © 2024 by Claudia Kielich

Cover by Eberle Arts

All rights reserved.

No part of this book may be reproduced in any form or by any electronic or mechanical means, including information storage and retrieval systems, without written permission from the author, except for the use of brief quotations in a book review.

Made in the USA
Columbia, SC
13 April 2025